AUDREY HEPBURN

D0912446

Published by TAJ Books International LLC 2012

5501 Kincross Lane

Charlotte, North Carolina, USA

28277

Reprinted 2013

www.tajbooks.com

www.tajminibooks.com

Copyright © 2012 TAJ Books International LLC

All rights reserved. No part of this publication may be reproduced, stored in a
retrieval system, or transmitted in any form or by any means, electronic, mechanical,
photocopying, recording, or otherwise, without the prior written permission of the
Publisher and copyright holders.

All notations of errors or omissions (author inquiries, permissions) concerning the
content of this book should be addressed to

info@tajbooks.com.

Research: Isabella Alston

ISBN 978-1-84406-201-0

978-1-62732-012-2 Paperback

Printed in China

3 4 5 16 15 14

AUDREY HEPBURN

T&J

KATHRYN DIXON

EARLY LIFE

Audrey Kathleen Ruston was born on Rue Keyenveld in Ixelles, a municipality in Brussels, Belgium, in the early morning hours of May 4, 1929. Her family had recently moved from London. The family surname was changed by Audrey's father to Hepburn-Ruston in homage to the Hepburn family name, which had recently died out. Audrey would later drop the Ruston surname.

Audrey was the only child of Joseph Victor Anthony Ruston (1889–1980), a Bohemian (the Czech Republic)-born Englishman of Irish, French, English, and Austrian descent with an erstwhile career in finance, and his second wife, Baroness Ella van Heemstra (1900–1984), a Dutch aristocrat, whose parents (Audrey's grandparents) were Baroness Elbrig van Asbeck and Baron Aernoud van Heemstra who had Dutch, Hungarian, and French heritage.

The Baron and Baroness van Heemstra traveled internationally in service to the Netherlands' Queen Wilhelmina. Audrey had two half-brothers by her mother's first marriage: Jonkheer Arnoud Robert Alexander Quarles van Ufford (1920–1979) and Jonkheer Ian Edgar Bruce Quarles van Ufford (1924–2010), known more succinctly as Alexander and Ian.

Soon after Audrey's birth, her mother began searching for a house in the country where her children could be raised in a quiet, calm, and beautiful environment. The baroness settled on a house located in Linkebeck, a small village located just a few miles outside of Brussels. It was here that Audrey spent the first six years of her life, years in which she would develop a very close, if somewhat unemotionally uninvolved, attachment to her mother.

With two older brothers, Audrey grew up a bit of a tomboy and took more interest playing outdoors and rough-housing with her brothers than she did playing with dolls indoors, like most girls of that age do. In addition, she showed an interest at an early age in theatre, music, and dance, often performing for her family.

Although born in Belgium, Audrey had British citizenship. From 1935 to 1938, Audrey attended Miss Rigden's School, a girls' boarding school in the village of Elham, Kent, in southeast England. It was here that Audrey was first introduced to the study of ballet.

In 1939, just as the horrors of World War II were being unleashed across Europe, Audrey, her mother, and two half-brothers moved to their maternal grandfather's home in Arnhem in the Netherlands, believing the neutrality of Holland would keep them out of harms way. Audrey's grandfather had served as the mayor of Arnhem, although his past position did not provide any measure of safety.

Audrey's father, in England at the time, put her on the last plane out of England to Holland on the day that England declared war on Germany. By this time, Audrey's parents had divorced. Her father, reputed to be a Nazi sympathizer, would not reunite with Audrey for another two decades. Mel Ferrer, Audrey's first husband, found her father in Dublin, Ireland, with the help of the Red Cross. Mel believed that Audrey was troubled by not having known her father. Even though father and daughter did not grow close after their reunion, Audrey supported him financially until his death.

While in Arnhem, Audrey attended the Arnhem Conservatory, training in ballet in addition to the standard school curriculum. After Germany invaded the Netherlands in 1940, worried that her name sounded too English and fearing the consequences of that, Audrey adopted the pseudonym Edda van Heemstra, a derivative of her mother's name, Ella. She could easily modify her mother's documents, changing "Ella" to "Edda."

During the war, Audrey and her mother did not know the whereabouts of her two brothers, Alexander and Ian. Alexander went underground and Ian was held by the Germans. Both survived their experiences, but were not reunited with the family until Germany's unconditional surrender, which occurred on May 4, 1945, Audrey's 16th birthday.

Having worked hard at her craft and having attained some proficiency as a ballerina, Audrey secretly danced for Dutch audiences to collect money for the Dutch resistance. She later said, "The best audience I ever had made not a single sound at the end of my performances." Eventually, the difficulties of the war took a toll on Audrey's health and she grew too weak to dance until the conclusion of the war.

Hepburn in a screen test for **Roman Holiday**, *also used as promotional material.*

In September 1944, Audrey's hometown of Arnhem was devastated by Allied artillery fire under Operation Market Garden, a failed attempt by western Allied forces to take the eight bridges spanning the Rhine and the system of canals that marked the Holland/German border. During the six-month-long Dutch famine that followed in the unusually severe winter of 1944–1945, known in Holland as the *Hongerwinter*, or Hunger Winter, the Germans blocked the resupply routes of the northern Netherlands' already-limited food and fuel supplies.

The German blockade was in retaliation for railway strikes encouraged by the exiled Dutch government and were intended to hinder the German occupation. As a result, the Dutch people in the north were literally starving (the southern Netherlands had been liberated soon after the Allied invasion on D-Day in June 1944) and Audrey was among them. Audrey suffered the effects of malnutrition for the remainder of her life.

Early Career

After WWII ended in 1945, Audrey moved to Amsterdam, where she took ballet lessons with Sonia Gaskell, eventually returning to England with her mother to live in London. Gaskell provided an introduction to Marie Rambert, reputed to have coached the world famous Russian ballet dancer Vaslav Nijinsky. Audrey studied ballet for a time at the Ballet Rambert, supporting herself with part-time work as a model. But because Audrey was tall for a prima ballerina at 5 feet 7 inches in height and still suffering the lingering effects of poor nutrition, Audrey had to face the fact that she should pursue a career other than as a professional ballerina. Feeling suited to performing, she turned to acting.

Audrey's mother—even though a baroness and descended from a long line of Dutch nobility—was forced to work menial jobs in order to support them. Audrey sought employment in acting and modeling, recalling later in life that "I needed the money; it paid 3 pounds more than ballet jobs." Her acting career began with the educational film Dutch in *Seven Lessons* (1948). As a London chorus girl, she played in the musical theatre production of *High Button Shoes* (1948), choreographed by Jerome Robbins, at the London Hippodrome as well as Cecil Landeau's musical revues *Sauce Tartare* (1949) and *Sauce Piquante* (1950) at the Cambridge Theatre in the West End, earning a featured role in *Sauce Piquante.* While working in the West End, Audrey appeared in small minor roles in the 1951 films *One Wild Oat*, *Laughter in Paradise*, *Young Wives' Tale*, *The Lavender Hill Mob*, and *The Secret People.* In *The Secret People*, Audrey performed two short dancing sequences in character as a ballerina.

During the filming of *Monte Carlo Baby* (1951), the French novelist Colette, who happened to be in Monte Carlo where the film was being shot, noticed Audrey, quickly recommending her to Anita Loos to play the title role in *Gigi*, the Broadway play she was adapting from the very popular film. When Colette approached Audrey about playing Gigi, Audrey replied modestly, "I'm sorry, Madame, but it is impossible. I wouldn't be able to, because I can't act." Nevertheless, *Gigi* opened on November 24, 1951, at the Fulton Theatre in New York City with Audrey Hepburn front and center, the

recipient of rave reviews. So fabulous, in fact, that her name was moved above the title of the play on the theater marquee before the next performance. *Gigi* ran for six months in front of a packed house.

In 1952, Hepburn was engaged to James Hanson, a fellow Brit, who would later become a major industrialist, becoming Lord Hanson after being knighted by Queen Elizabeth II in 1976. Hanson, along with Audrey's mother, attended the opening performance of *Gigi*. The engagement would be broken soon, however, with Audrey blaming their busy schedules as too onerous to make for a happy marriage.

Hepburn's first starring role was in the Italian-set *Roman Holiday* (1953) as Princess Anne, a "bored and sheltered" European princess who, after escaping her guardians, falls in love with American newsman Gregory Peck. Producers initially wanted Elizabeth Taylor for the role but after Hepburn's screen test, director William Wyler was so impressed that he cast her in the lead. Following the screen test, the camera kept rolling while Hepburn, displaying her ability, candidly answered questions, relaxed and unaware that she was still being filmed. Wyler

later commented, "She had everything I was looking for: charm, innocence and talent. She also was very funny. She was absolutely enchanting and we said, 'That's the girl!'" The instant celebrity that came with Roman Holiday put Audrey Hepburn, featured in her role as Princess Anne, on the September 1953 cover of *TIME* magazine. Even though Audrey was engaged to be married to James Hanson at the time, rumors abounded that Audrey and Gregory Peck were romantically involved, but both denied it.

Audrey garnered critical and commercial acclaim for her portrayal of the elusive princess and supplemented her Academy Award win with her first BAFTA Award for Best Actress in a Leading Role and Golden Globe Award for Best Actress, Motion Picture Drama. Returning to America after filming *Roman Holiday* in Italy for four months, Audrey returned to *Gigi*, taking the play on the road for eight months, ending up in Los Angeles and San Francisco in the last month. Paramount signed Audrey to a seven-picture contract with 12 months between

Audrey Hepburn was engaged to James Hanson in 1952. He later became a Lord and a major British industrialist.

Colette, the French novelist, discovered Audrey Hepburn for the role of Gigi on Broadway.

films so that she could continue her work in live theater.

It was during the filming of *Roman Holiday* that Audrey met Connie Wald, the then-wife of Jerry Wald, a Hollywood film producer. Connie, who called Audrey "Ruby," was to become Audrey's dearest girlfriend whom she would visit in Los Angeles innumerable times throughout her life and with whom she would stay during the last months before her death, before she went back to Switzerland for

her last Christmas in 1993. Audrey and her family called Connie's home their "home away from home."

Following *Roman Holiday*, Audrey starred in Billy Wilder's romantic comedy *Sabrina* (1954) in which the wealthy Larrabee brothers, played by Humphrey Bogart and William Holden, compete for the affections of their chauffeur's innocent daughter, Sabrina, who is played by Audrey. Life imitates art and, during the filming of *Sabrina*, Audrey

and the already-married William Holden did become romantically involved, but nothing was to come of it. For her performance, she was nominated for the 1955 Academy Award for Best Actress and won the BAFTA Award for Best Actress in a Leading Role that same year.

The uncredited Hubert de Givenchy was responsible for many of Audrey's outfits in the film. Edith Head, who received sole billing for costume design, won the Oscar for her efforts. In *Breakfast at*

Tiffany's, Givenchy would share credit with Head. Givenchy and Audrey's collaboration in Sabrina developed into a life-long friendship that benefited them both. Audrey Hepburn was, and is still, synonymous with exquisite, tasteful style. That style was largely orchestrated by Givenchy and carried off unerringly by Audrey's character and intelligence. In 1957, Givenchy even created a perfume that he called L'Interdit, the French word for "Forbidden," which was inspired by

Audrey. Givenchy remained Hepburn's friend and ambassador, and she his muse, throughout her life.

That same year, 1954, Audrey starred in Jean Giraudoux's *Ondine* on Broadway with Mel Ferrer. He had orchestrated the joint appearance, having fallen in love with Audrey after meeting her at a cocktail party hosted by Gregory Peck, her co-star in *Roman Holiday*. Although still married to his wife Frances at the time, Mel believed he and Audrey could follow in the footsteps of Olivier and Leigh or Lunt and Fontaine.

Audrey and Mel began living together in Greenwich Village shortly after the *Ondine* rehearsals began. But after 157 performances, the play was forced to close because Audrey was in a state of exhaustion, smoking a pack of cigarettes a day and 15 pounds underweight. Just 24 years old, Audrey was "generating more excitement than Marilyn Monroe." Regardless, Audrey's performance in *Ondine* won her the 1954 Tony Award for Best Performance by a Leading Actress in a Play.

Having only known each other for eight months, Audrey and Mel Ferrer married on September 24, 1954, in Switzerland

Audrey Hepburn and Gregory Peck in Roman Holiday.

close to Lake Lucerne, and set up housekeeping in the nearby village of Bürgenstock. Audrey and Mel were to experience two miscarriages before the birth of their son, Sean Hepburn Ferrer, on July 17, 1960. The second miscarriage occurred when Audrey was filming *The Unforgiven* in Mexico with the director

John Huston. Audrey fell off a horse, breaking vertebrae in her back, and eventually lost the baby after completing the film and returning to Switzerland.

Mel had four other children, two by each of his two previous wives: Frances Pilchard, whom he married twice, and Barbara Tripp.

By the mid-1950s, both a huge motion picture and Broadway star, Audrey was also a major style maker and trend setter, appearing on the covers of *Vogue* and *Harper's Bazaar.* Her elfin-like appearance and refined sense of chic were admired and imitated around the world.

Previous page, right: Audrey and Mel Ferrer on their wedding day in Switzerland.
Right: Audrey Hepburn, Humphrey Bogart, and William Holden in Sabrina.
Above: As Sabrina, pre-Paris.
Right: As Sabrina, post-Paris.

Audrey, in character as Sabrina, spying on her crush, the younger Larrabee brother, played by William Holden.

In 1955, she was awarded the Golden Globe for World Film Favorite, Female. Now one of Hollywood's most popular box-office attractions, she went on to star in a series of successful films during the remainder of the decade, including her BAFTA- and Golden Globe-nominated role as Natasha Rostova in *War and Peace* (1956), an adaptation of the Tolstoy novel set during the Napoleonic wars, with her then-husband Mel Ferrer and Henry Fonda.

In 1957, Audrey again returned to her ballet roots, debuting in the musical film *Funny Face* with Fred Astaire. She also starred alongside Gary Cooper

and Maurice Chevalier in the romantic comedy *Love in the Afternoon*, directed by the legendary director Billy Wilder. Wilder once said of her: "Audrey Hepburn, single-handed, may make bosoms a thing of the past."

Venturing into the medium of TV, Audrey and Mel Ferrer acted together in the BBC movie *Mayerling,* which recalls the true and tragic story of the apparent murder-suicide of Crown Prince Rudolf of Austria and his lover Baroness Mary Vetsera, played by Audrey. Rudolf was the only son of Emperor Franz Josef I of Austria and Empress Elisabeth, and heir to the throne of the combined Austrian-Hungarian Empire. Rudolf's mistress was the daughter of the late Baron Albin Vetsera, a diplomat at the Austrian court.

The bodies of the 30-year-old Archduke and the 17-year-old Baroness were discovered in the Imperial hunting lodge at Mayerling in the Vienna Woods, 15 miles southwest of Vienna, on the morning of January 30, 1889. Because Rudolf died without a son, upon his

Audrey with her co-star William Holden in Sabrina. *Audrey wears a dress designed by Hubert de Givenchy.*

father's death, succession passed to Franz Joseph's brother, Karl Ludwig, and his issue, Archduke Franz Ferdinand, who would be assassinated along with his wife Sophie by Gavrillo Princip, a Serbian nationalist, at Sarajevo in June 1914, a catalyst for the First World War.

Given Audrey's European heritage and aristocratic lineage, she was thus perfectly fitted to step into the shoes of Mary Vetsara. In fact, after meeting Audrey, the Queen Mother reportedly told her daughter Queen Elizabeth II: "She is one of us."

The Nun's Story (1959), in which Audrey starred alongside Peter Finch, earned her a third Academy Award nomination and another BAFTA Award. Audrey also won

the 1959 New York Film Critics Circle Best Actress Award for *The Nun's Story*, but was unable to pick up the award herself. Her friend, Elizabeth Taylor, did the honors for her.

The *Films in Review* critic Harry Hart applauded her performance in *The Nun's Story*, stating that it "will forever silence those who have thought her less an actress than a symbol of the sophisticated child-woman. In *The Nun's Story*, Miss Hepburn reveals the kind of acting talent that can project inner feelings of both depth and complexity so skillfully you must scrutinize her intently on a second and third viewing of the film to perceive how she does it. Her portrayal of Sister Luke is one of the great performances of the screen."

Audrey next starred with the 26-year-old Anthony Perkins, a younger leading man than Audrey had worked with before, in the exotically romantic adventure *Green Mansions*, released in 1959, based on the novel by W.H. Hudson. The film was directed by Mel Ferrer. *Green Mansions* was panned at the box office,

Left: With Henry Fonda in War and Peace.
Right: With Mel Ferrer in War and Peace.

Audrey as Natasha Rostova in War in Peace, 1956.

but three months later, *The Nun's Story* was released to great acclaim, diverting attention from the disappointment of *Green Mansions*.

In 1960, Audrey appeared alongside Burt Lancaster and Lillian Gish in *The Unforgiven*, her only Western film. It was not considered a triumph by almost any count.

Audrey was heavily pregnant with her first son Sean when she was approached about the role of Holly Golightly, which ironically produced the iconically thin image of Audrey. In 1961, Audrey began work on Blake Edwards' *Breakfast at Tiffany's*, a film loosely based on the Truman Capote novella. The film was

drastically changed from the original version to be more acceptable to the viewing public. Gone from the film was the implication of impropriety in Holly's occupation, her unwanted pregnancy, and subsequent miscarriage. In went the ring from Tiffany. Capote disapproved of many changes and proclaimed that Hepburn was "grossly miscast" as Holly Golightly, a role he had envisioned for Marilyn Monroe. In fact, Capote had envisioned himself in the role of George Peppard until Marty Jurow, the co-producer of the film, deftly persuaded him otherwise.

Audrey's portrayal of Holly Golightly was nominated for the 1962 Academy Award for Best Actress. Even the composer, Henry Mancini, of the film's theme "Moon River," enthused about Audrey's command over her interpretation of Holly Golightly, saying that "'Moon River' was written for her. No one else had ever understood it so completely." Often considered her defining role, Audrey's high-fashion style and sophistication as Holly Golightly became synonymous with her. She considered the role "the jazziest of my career."

Audrey and her then-husband Mel Ferrer in **War and Peace** *for which she would garner several best actress nominations.*

The "little black dress" worn by Audrey as Holly Golightly at the opening of the film is unquestionably one of the most iconic items of clothing in the history of the twentieth century. The "quintessential" dress was sold for $807,000 in 2006 with the proceeds going to City of Joy Aid, a charity benefitting the poor in India. It is the highest price paid for a dress from a film. The dress auctioned by Christie's was not, however, the one that Audrey wore in the film. Of the two dresses that Hepburn did wear, one is stored in the Givenchy archives and the other is displayed in the Museum of Costume in Madrid.

Forty years after Audrey wore the Givenchy-designed dress in *Breakfast at Tiffany's*, the dress topped a list of the greatest screen outfits. Absolutely a testament to Audrey's beguiling personality, she "truly made that little black dress a fashion staple which has stood the test of time despite competition from some of the most stylish females around."

Playing opposite Shirley MacLaine and James Garner, Audrey's next role was in William Wyler's drama *The Children's Hour*, released in1961, originally a play written by Lillian Hellman. Hepburn

Above and right: With Gary Cooper in Love in the Afternoon.

and MacLaine play the owners of a girl's school who are accused by a student of a lesbian relationship. The film was one of Hollywood's earliest treatments of the subject and, as such, was approached gingerly and subtly. The film and Hepburn's performance went seemingly unnoticed both critically and commercially. Bosley Crowther of *The New York Times* noted, however, that "it is not too well acted, except by Audrey Hepburn" who "gives the impression of being sensitive and pure" of its "muted theme."

Audrey's only film with Cary Grant was the comic thriller *Charade,* which opened in 1963. Audrey, who played Regina

Lampert, finds herself pursued by several men (including Grant) who are chasing the fortune her murdered husband had stolen. The role earned her a third and final competitive BAFTA Award and another Golden Globe nomination. Grant was 59 years old at the time and Hepburn was 34. Audrey was Grant's 50th leading

Below: Audrey Hepburn in the Congo for the filming of The Nun's Story.
Right: Audrey as Sister Luke.

lady. Of her, Grant once said, "All I want for Christmas is another picture with Audrey Hepburn."

In 1964, *Paris When It Sizzles* re-teamed Audrey with William Holden nearly 10 years after *Sabrina.* The comedy, set in Paris, has Audrey playing Gabrielle Simpson, the young assistant of a Hollywood screenwriter, played by Holden, who is late in delivering a contracted script due to writer's block. The film was not popular with critics, one of whom characterized it as "marshmallow-weight hokum." Behind the scenes, the set was plagued with problems: Holden tried, without success, to rekindle a romance with the now-married actress, while he struggled desperately with alcoholism. The problem was so bad that the film's director, Richard Quine, finally persuaded Holden to spend a week in rehab, even before shooting was completed.

Being rather superstitious, Audrey requested dressing room 55, which was the dressing room she used for her two earlier smash hits: *Roman Holiday* and *Breakfast at Tiffany's.* Unfortunately, the magic had worn off because critics "uniformly panned" the movie. The original cinematographer was Claude

Renoir, the grandson of the Impressionist painter Pierre-Auguste Renoir, but after seeing what she felt were unflattering dailies, Audrey asked that he be removed. He was replaced by Charles Lang, who had photographed Audrey in her role as Sabrina. Once again, Givenchy designed Audrey's costumes. Having created a perfume in her honor, L'Interdit, she asked that his credit in the film include her perfume in addition to her costumes.

Audrey next landed the role of Eliza in George Cukor's film adaptation of *My Fair Lady*, the 1954 musical theater production starring Julie Andrews and Rex Harrison, based on George Bernard Shaw's play *Pygmaylion*. Rex Harrison reprised his role, but it was thought that Julie Andrews was too much of an unknown to carry the film. Audrey sought the role through her agent Kurt Frings who ultimately won her a $1 million salary and a percentage of the gross, almost unheard of at the time.

Audrey did not have a strong singing voice so her originally recorded vocals were replaced with those of Marni Nixon. Interestingly, Rex Harrison didn't sing either and would half-speak, half-sing his songs, just as he did on stage opposite Julie Andrews. Audrey studied closely

with a voice coach to thoroughly master Eliza's Cockney accent. Costumes, sets, and production design for *My Fair Lady* were by Cecil Beaton, whose work Audrey adored. Her record salary paid dividends in gaining the audience's attention, but not so much that of the critics. Audrey did not earn an Oscar nomination for her performance, although she did win the New York Film Critics Circle Best Actress

Award in 1964 for her role as Eliza. Sparking rumors of conflict between the two actresses, Julie Andrews was nominated and won an Oscar for best actress in 1964 for *Mary Poppins*, proving that she may have been able to carry off Eliza after all.

In the 1966 heist comedy *How to Steal a Million*, Audrey played Nicole, the daughter of a famous art collector whose collection consists entirely of forgeries. Fearing her father's exposure as a forger, Nicole sets out to steal one of his priceless statues with the help of Simon Dermott played by Peter O'Toole. Over time, *How to Steal a Million* has been noted more for Audrey's Givenchy-designed couture than for her performance.

In 1967, Audrey starred in two films: *Two for the Road* and *Wait Until Dark*.

The former, a nonlinear and innovative British comedy drama, traces the course of a troubled marriage and was directed by Stanley Donen. She starred opposite Albert Finney and was nominated for a Golden Globe, Best Actress in a Musical or Comedy, for her efforts.

Wait Until Dark, an edgy thriller in which Audrey demonstrated her acting range by playing the part of a terrorized blind woman, would earn her three best actress nominations, although no win. The movie was produced by Mel Ferrer, but filmed on the brink of their divorce, proved to be a trying and stressful experience for Audrey. Alan Arkin co-starred.

Immediately after completing *Wait Until Dark*, Audrey disappeared into seclusion. Her marriage to Mel Ferrer was in its final months.

LATE CAREER

From 1967 onward, after 15 highly successful years in film, Audrey chose to devote more time to her family, taking a hiatus from her professional career for almost the next 10 years. Her first son, Sean Ferrer, was 7 years old. She was entering her last year of marriage to Mel Ferrer. After a marriage of 14 years, Mr. and Mrs. Mel Ferrer were officially divorced on December 5, 1968.

While relaxing on a Mediterranean cruise as a guest of her friends the millionaire Paul Weiller and his wife, Princess Olympia Torlonia, Audrey met Italian psychiatrist Andrea Dotti, nine years her junior. Initially concerned about the age difference and her status as a divorcee, Audrey nevertheless fell in love and the couple was married on January 18, 1969, in Morges, Switzerland.

At age 40, Audrey gave birth to their son, Luca, on February 8, 1970. During her pregnancy Audrey rested in Switzerland in an effort to forego another miscarriage. During her time away from Rome, where her husband Andrea maintained his practice of psychiatry specializing in the treatment of drug addiction, rumors—fueled by photos of his dalliances with beautiful women—began to swirl.

Audrey was accepted wholeheartedly by Andrea's family and tried to adapt to her role as the wife of an Italian man who felt it his right to have female relationships outside of his marriage, even though he had captured the love and admiration of one of the most accomplished and desirable women in the world, Audrey Hepburn.

The marriage lasted 13 years, officially ending in 1982, although Audrey began a relationship with the Dutch actor Robert Wolders, the widower of actress Merle Oberon, in 1980. Robert Wolders would be Audrey's loving companion until her

Left: Promotion for The Children's Hour. *Right: Audrey and Shirley MacLaine starred together in a screen adaption of Lillian Hellman's play* The Children's Hour *in 1961.*

death in 1993. In the last years of WWII, although Robby (as Audrey called him) lived near her family in a suburb of Arnhem, they did not know each other. Nevertheless, their shared childhood experiences bonded them.

Audrey returned to films in 1976, co-starring with Sean Connery, in the period piece *Robin and Marian*, which was only moderately successful. After being away from films for almost a decade, her appearance at the New York opening of *Robin and Marian* at Radio City Music Hall was greeted by roughly 6,000 fans cheering her return to the big screen.

In 1979, Audrey took the lead role of Elizabeth Roffe in the international production of *Bloodline*, re-teaming with director Terence Young with whom she had worked in *Wait Until Dark*. She shared top billing with co-stars Ben Gazzara, James Mason, and Romy Schneider. Author Sidney Sheldon revised his novel when it was reissued to tie into the film, making her character a much older woman to better match the actress's age. The film, an international intrigue amid the jet-set, was a critical and box office failure.

On the set of *Bloodline*, Audrey and her co-star Ben Gazzara began a romance that lasted only a couple of years. Because of her attraction to Gazzara, Audrey accepted her last starring role in a cinematic film, the 1981 comedy *They All Laughed* directed by Peter Bogdanovich, Gazzara's friend. Gazzara was also signed for the film.

The film was plagued by misfortune. It was supposed to be Bogdanovich's comeback after a string of poorly performing movies. Bogdanovich had

Above: Walter Mathau in Charade.
Right: Audrey Hepburn in Charade.
Next page, left: Audrey with Julie Andrews on the night Julie won best actress for her 1964 performance in Mary Poppins. *Audrey was not nominated for* My Fair Lady, *sparking rumors of jealousy—which were denied—between the two actresses.*

Left: Audrey in My Fair Lady *with Rex Harrison as Henry Higgins.*
Right: With Peter O'Toole in How to Steal a Million.

blown into movies in 1971 with *The Last Picture Show*, quickly followed the popular *What's Up Doc?* and critically acclaimed *Paper Moon.* Unfortunately, before its release, *They All Laughed* was overshadowed by the murder of one of its stars, Bogdanovich's girlfriend, Dorothy Stratten. The film was eventually released after Stratten's death but only in limited runs.

In 1987, Audrey co-starred with Robert Wagner in the tongue-in-cheek made-for-television caper film *Love Among Thieves*, which borrowed elements from several of her earlier films, most notably *Charade* and *How to Steal a Million.*

After finishing her last role in a motion picture in 1988, a cameo appearance as an angel in Steven Spielberg's *Always*,

Audrey completed only two more entertainment-related projects, both critically acclaimed for which she received posthumous recognition.

Gardens of the World with Audrey Hepburn was a PBS documentary television series, her final performance before cameras filmed on location in seven countries in the spring and summer of 1990. A one-hour special, broadcast in March 1991, preceded the series for which Audrey was posthumously awarded an Emmy for Outstanding Individual Achievement-Informational Programming in 1993. The series commenced the day after her death on January 21, 1993.

Recorded in 1992, her spoken word album, *Audrey Hepburn's Enchanted Tales,* features readings of classic children's stories. It earned her a posthumous Grammy Award for Best Spoken Word Album for Children.

Audrey is one of the few entertainers to posthumously win Grammy and Emmy Awards.

FILMOGRAPHY

IMBD lists 31 film credits for Audrey Hepburn. Audrey had minor roles in six films and two TV series in 1951 and 1952. Her breakout role in 1953 was Princess Anne in *Roman Holiday*, for which she won the Oscar for Best Actress, opposite Gregory Peck. Next, in 1954, Audrey played the title character in *Sabrina*, co-starring with Humphrey Bogart and William Holden.

Audrey then worked steadily in films until 1967 when she starred as the recently blinded young woman Susy Hendrix in *Wait Until Dark*. In 1979, Audrey returned to film as Lady Marian in *Robin and Marian*, a tale of an aging Robin Hood and his life-long love. She would act in only three more films, ending her professional acting career in 1989 with a cameo role as an angel in Stephen Spielberg's *Always*.

In addition to her Oscar win as Best Actress in 1953, Audrey was nominated four other times for her work in *Sabrina*, *The Nun's Story*, *Breakfast at Tiffany's*, and *Wait Until Dark*. Her preparation for *The Nun's Story* took Audrey a year's time and 14,000 miles. She claimed that she gave more of her "time, energy, and thought" to her role as Sister Luke than to any of her previous roles. Audrey's ballet training was put to good use in both *The Secret People* and *Funny Face*, dancing toe-to-toe with Fred Astaire in the latter film.

Above: With Alan Arkin in Wait Until Dark.
Right: With Rex Harrison in My Fair Lady.

61

Year Released	Title	Role
1989	*Always*	Hap
1987	*Love Among Thieves* (TV movie)	Baroness Caroline DuLac
1981	*They All Laughed*	Angela Niotes
1979	*Bloodline*	Elizabeth Roffe
1976	*Robin and Marian*	Lady Marian
1967	*Wait Until Dark*	Susy Hendrix
1967	*Two for the Road*	Joanna Wallace
1966	*How to Steal a Million*	Nicole
1964	*My Fair Lady*	Eliza Doolittle
1964	*Paris When It Sizzles*	Gabrielle Simpson/Gaby
1963	*Charade*	Regina Lampert
1961	*The Children's Hour*	Karen Wright
1961	*Breakfast at Tiffany's*	Holly Golightly
1960	*The Unforgiven*	Rachel Zachary
1959	*The Nun's Story*	Sister Luke (Gabrielle van der Mal)
1959	*Green Mansions*	Rima
1957	*Love in the Afternoon*	Ariane Chavasse/Thin Girl
1957	*Funny Face*	Jo Stockton
1957	*Mayerling* (TV movie)	Marie Vetsera
1956	*War and Peace*	Natasha Rostova
1954	*Sabrina*	Sabrina Fairchild
1953	*We Go to Monte Carlo*	Linda Farrel
1953	*Roman Holiday*	Princess Anne
1952	*The Secret People*	Nora Brentano
1951	*Young Wives' Tale*	Eve Lester
1951	*We Will All Go to Monte Carlo*	Melissa Walter
1951	*The Silent Village* (BBCTV movie)	Celia
1951	*The Lavender Hill Mob*	Chiquita
1951	*Laughter in Paradise*	Frieda, the cigarette girl
1951	*One Wild Oat*	Hotel receptionist

Marriage to Andrea Dotti on January 18, 1969, in Morges, Switzerland.

LEADING MEN

From very early in her career, Audrey Hepburn worked opposite the crème de la crème of male leads. Eight of her co-stars earned Best Actor Oscars in their lifetimes: Gregory Peck, Humphrey Bogart, William Holden, Henry Fonda, Gary Cooper, Peter Finch, Burt Lancaster, and Rex Harrison. Others were nominated for the Best Actor Oscar, but didn't get the nod. Included in this category are Peter O'Toole, Alan Arkin, Cary Grant, James Garner, and Albert Finney.

Audrey acted with her husband, Mel Ferrer, in two movies: one for the big screen, *War and Peace*, and one for television, *Mayerling.* Mel Ferrer was Audrey's husband from 1954 to 1968.

A second love interest with whom she worked was Ben Gazzara. According to Gazzara's memoir, *In the Moment*, he and Audrey, having met on the set of *Bloodline* in 1979, were romantically involved for a time. In 1981, they starred together in the movie *They All Laughed*, written and directed by Peter Bogdanovich.

Reportedly, Audrey had a fling with William Holden while they were filming *Sabrina*. Holden was married at the time, complicating the relationship. The two would work together again 10 years later in *Paris When It Sizzles.* Although both Audrey and Holden were married then, Holden tried to re-ignite the flame, but was wholly unsuccessful.

A U D R E Y   H E P B U R N

Year Released	Title	Leading Man
1987	*Love Among Thieves* (TV movie)	Robert Wagner
1981	*They All Laughed*	Ben Gazzara
1979	*Bloodline*	Ben Gazzara
1976	*Robin and Marian*	Sean Connery
1967	*Wait Until Dark*	Alan Arkin
1967	*Two for the Road*	Albert Finney
1966	*How to Steal a Million*	Peter O'Toole
1964	*My Fair Lady*	Rex Harrison
1964	*Paris When It Sizzles*	William Holden
1963	*Charade*	Cary Grant
1961	*The Children's Hour*	James Garner
1961	*Breakfast at Tiffany's*	George Peppard
1960	*The Unforgiven*	Burt Lancaster
1959	*The Nun's Story*	Peter Finch
1959	*Green Mansions*	Anthony Perkins
1957	*Love in the Afternoon*	Gary Cooper
1957	*Funny Face*	Fred Astaire
1957	*Mayerling* (TV movie)	Mel Ferrer
1956	*War and Peace*	Henry Fonda & Mel Ferrer
1954	*Sabrina*	Humphrey Bogart & William Holden
1953	*Roman Holiday*	Gregory Peck

Awards and Honors

Audrey Hepburn was liberally showered with well-deserved awards and recognition throughout her life in honor of her professional acumen and her humanitarian outreach. The number of awards received by Audrey is so great that only selected honors are highlighted in the following list of her achievements.

Audrey is one of only a handful of artists, 10 to be exact, who have been awarded, on a competitive basis, an Oscar, Tony, Emmy, and Grammy. In 1953, Audrey won a Best Actress Oscar for *Roman Holiday*. She won a Tony in 1954 for Best Dramatic Actress in *Ondine*, an Emmy in 1993 for Outstanding Achievement-Informational Programming for a one-hour special preceding the PBS TV series *Gardens of the World with Audrey Hepburn*, and a Grammy in 1993 for her recording of a children's book.

The Emmy and Grammy were awarded posthumously in the year of her death.

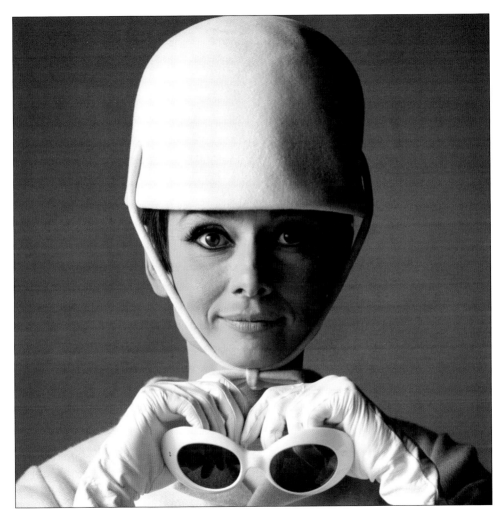

FILM

1952

Best Debut Performance by an Actress for *Gigi* given by Billboard, The Donaldson Award for Outstanding Achievement in Theatre

1953

One of America's Five Most Promising Newcomers given by *Photoplay* Magazine

1954

BAFTA Best Film Actress Award (1953) for *Roman Holiday* given by the British Academy of Film and Television Arts

Golden Globe Award: Best Motion Picture Actress, Drama (1953) for *Roman Holiday* given by Hollywood Foreign Press Association

Academy Award: Oscar, Best Actress (1953) for *Roman Holiday* given by the Academy of Motion Pictures Arts and Sciences

Tony Award: Best Dramatic Actress for *Ondine* given by The American Theatre Wing and The League of American Theatres and Producers

1955

NYFCC Best Actress Nomination (1954), BAFTA Best Film Actress Nomination (1954), and Academy Award: Oscar Nomination, Best Actress for *Sabrina*

Golden Globe Henrietta Award: World Film Favorite, Female, given by the Hollywood Foreign Press Association

1956

Victoire du Cinéma Francais Award

Modern Screen Award: Best Performance for *War and Peace*

1957

NYFCC Best Actress Nomination (1956); BAFTA Best Film Actress Nomination (1956); and Golden Globe Nomination: Best Motion Picture Actress, Drama (1956) for *War and Peace*

1958

Golden Globe Nomination: Best Motion Picture Actress, Musical/Comedy (1957) and NYFCC Best Actress Nomination (1957) for *Love in the Afternoon*

1959

Zulueta Prize: Best Actress for *The Nun's Story* given by the San Sebastian International Film Festival

Best Film Actress of 1959 given by the Variety Club of Great Britain

1960

Hollywood Walk of Fame Star, Motion Picture Category, on 1650 Vine Street in Hollywood, CA

NYFCC Best Actress Award (1959); BAFTA Best Film Actress Award (1959); Academy Award: Oscar Nomination, Best Actress; and Golden Globe Nomination: Best Motion Picture Actress, Drama (1959) for *The Nun's Story*

David di Donatello Best Foreign Actress Award for *The Nun's Story* given by Accademia del Cinema Italiano

1962

Golden Globe Nomination: Best Motion Picture Actress, Musical/Comedy (1961); David di Donatello Best Foreign Actress Award; and Academy Awards: Oscar Nomination, Best Actress (1961) for *Breakfast at Tiffany's*

1964

Golden Globe Nomination: Best Motion Picture Actress, Musical/ Comedy (1963) for *Charade*

Victoire du Cinéma Francais Award

1965

NYFCC Best Actress Award (1964); David di Donatello Best Foreign Actress Award; and Golden Globe Nomination: Best Motion Picture Actress, Musical/Comedy (1964) for *My Fair Lady*

BAFTA Best Film Actress Award (1963) for *Charade*

President Reagan talking with Audrey Hepburn and Robert Wolders at a private dinner for the Prince of Wales at the White House.

1968

NYFCC Best Actress Award Nomination (1967); Golden Globe Nomination: Best Motion Picture Actress, Drama (1967); and Academy Award: Oscar Nomination, Best Actress for *Wait Until Dark*
Golden Globe Nomination: Best Motion

Picture Actress, Musical/Comedy (1967) for *Two for the Road*

Special Tony Award given by The American Theatre Wing and The League of American Theatres and Producers

1987

Commandeur de L'Ordre des Arts et des Lettres for significant contributions to furthering the arts in France and throughout the world presented by the French Minister of Culture and Communications

1990

Cecil B. DeMille Award: Golden Globe Lifetime Achievement given by the Hollywood Foreign Press Association

1991

Gala Tribute Honoree named by the Film Society of Lincoln Center

1992

BAFTA Lifetime Achievement Award
George Eastman Award for distinguished contribution to the art of film

1993

SAG Lifetime Achievement Award given by the Screen Actors Guild of America

Emmy Award: Outstanding Individual Achievement

1999

American Film Institute Award: #3 Female Film Legend

In 1993, Audrey Hepburn was the 29th Life Achievement Recipient of the Screen Actors Guild Awards.

HUMANITARIAN

1976

Humanitarian Award for contributions to the world of motion pictures and charitable efforts on behalf of all children of all nations given by Variety, the Children's Charity of New York

1988

The International Danny Kaye Award for Children presented by the U.S. Committee for UNICEF

1989

International Humanitarian Award presented for the first time in history by the Institute for Human Understanding

Prix d' Humanite Award

Seventh Annual UNICEF Ball was in honor of Audrey Hepburn

1992

Presidential Medal of Freedom bestowed by Pres. George H.W. Bush

1993

Jean Hersholt Humanitarian Award (1992) Oscar accepted by Sean H. Ferrer given by the Academy of Motion Pictures Arts and Science

The Pearl S. Buck Woman's Award given by The Pearl S. Buck Foundation

International Humanitarian Award: "A Special Woman"

2002

"The Spirit of Audrey," a bronze sculpture by sculptor John Kennedy, located in the public plaza at UNICEF headquarters in New York City

Audrey Hepburn in Africa as goodwill ambassador for UNICEF.

STYLE AND FASHION

1961

Audrey was named to the International Best-Dressed Hall of Fame in 1961. Preceding Audrey in recognition, the winners in 1960 included H.R.H. The Duchess of Kent, H.R.H. Princess Grace of Monaco (nee Grace Kelly) who in 1964 would win the Best Actress Oscar after both she and Audrey were nominated, and Merle Oberon, an Indian-born British actress, whose fourth and last husband, Robert Wolders, widowed by her in 1979 became Audrey's companion from 1980 until her death in 1993.

In 1962, the year following Audrey's addition to the best-dressed list, the Parisian fashion designer Comtesse Jacqueline de Ribes was bestowed the honor.

Also sharing the honor with Audrey in the years since the list was begun by Eleanor Lambert in 1940, and inherited at her death by *Vanity Fair* magazine, are Wallis Simpson (Duchess of Windsor) in 1958, Jacqueline Kennedy Onassis in 1965, international singer and superstar Tina Turner in 1996, *Vogue* editor-in-chief Anna Wintour in 1997, and Nicole Kidman in 2004.

In 2011, the honor was bestowed on Kate Middleton, the Duchess of Cambridge, who shares Audrey's British heritage.

1992

Lifetime-of-Style Award given by the Council of Fashion Designers of America

The statue "The Spirit of Audrey" in the James P. Grant Plaza in New York City.

The plaque on the sculpture reads:

"THE SPIRIT OF AUDREY"
BY JOHN KENNEDY

DEDICATED TO THE MEMORY OF
AUDREY HEPBURN

UNICEF AMBASSADOR 1987-1993

DONATED BY ROBERT WOLDERS

OTHER

1959

Street Dedication: "Audrey Hepburn Laan" (Audrey Hepburn Lane) in Doorn, Netherlands

1990

"Audrey Hepburn Tulip" unveiled at Huis Doorn, Netherlands

One of the "50 Most Beautiful People in the World"

1993

Grammy Award: Best Spoken Word Album for Children for *Enchanted Tales*

2003

"Legends of Hollywood" U.S. Postage Stamp created by the U.S. Postal Service

2004

"Most Naturally Beautiful Woman of All Time" as named by an Evian-organized poll of an international panel of experts made up of beauty editors, make-up artists, fashion editors, model agencies, and fashion photographers

The Audrey Hepburn tulip.

QUOTES ATTRIBUTED TO AUDREY

"Nothing is impossible. The word itself says 'I'm possible'!"

"True friends are families which you can select."

"The best thing to hold onto in life is each other."

"Happy girls are the prettiest."

"There are certain shades of limelight that can wreck a girl's complexion."

"I've been lucky. Opportunities don't often come along. So, when they do, you have to grab them."

"Living is like tearing through a museum. Not until later do you really start absorbing what you saw, thinking about it, looking it up in a book, and remembering, because you can't take it in all at once."

"Paris is always a good idea."

"I was born with an enormous need for affection, and a terrible need to give it."

"I have to be alone very often. I'd be quite happy if I spent from Saturday night until Monday morning alone in my apartment. That's how I refuel."

Audrey Hepburn with President Carter
at a UNICEF event in 1990.

The following poem was cobbled together by Audrey from a letter that the author Sam Levenson wrote to his granddaughter at her birth. Audrey loved the message so much that she read her version to her family on Christmas Eve 1993, her last Christmas. Her son Sean Ferrer then read the poem as a tribute to Audrey at the close of her funeral service.

TIME-TESTED BEAUTY TIPS

For attractive lips, speak words of kindness.
For lovely eyes, seek out the good in people.
For a slim figure, share your food with the hungry.
For beautiful hair, let a child run his fingers through it once a day.
For poise, walk with the knowledge you'll never walk alone.
We leave you a tradition with a future. The tender loving care of human beings will never become obsolete.

People, even more than things, have to be restored, renewed, revived,
reclaimed and redeemed and redeemed and redeemed.
Never throw out anybody. Remember, if you ever need a helping hand, you'll find one at the end of your arm.
As you grow older you will discover that you have two hands: one for helping yourself, the other for helping others.
Your "good old days" are still ahead of you, may you have many of them.

LEGACY

The photographer Leo Fuchs said of Audrey that she "was a singular person. There ain't many like her.... She certainly was beautiful. She was very enticing at all times. She was a talented actress, and very personable."

Audrey's legacy as an actress and a humanitarian has been acknowledged in multiple ways during the last years of her life and in the years after her death. In 1999, the American Film Institute named her third among the Greatest Female Stars of All Time. In 2003, the U.S. Postal Service created a stamp in her honor as part of the series "Legends of Hollywood." And in 2004, almost a decade after her death, Audrey was named the "Most Naturally Beautiful Woman of All Time" by an international panel of beauty and fashion experts.

Audrey was the recipient of four posthumous awards: the 1993 Jean Hersholt Humanitarian Award given by The Academy of Motion Picture Arts and Sciences, the 1993 Screen Actors Guild Lifetime Achievement Award, and competitive Grammy and Emmy Awards.

A number of biographies have been penned about her since her death, including the loving memoir written by her son Sean Ferrer entitled *Audrey Hepburn, An Enchanted Spirit.* The 2000 dramatization of Audrey's life, *The Audrey Hepburn Story,* starred Jennifer Love Hewitt and Emmy Rossum as the older and younger Hepburn, respectively. The film concludes with footage of the real Audrey Hepburn, shot during one of her final missions for UNICEF.

Audrey was self-deprecating in describing her allure. She told Barbara Walters in 1989, "My look is attainable. Women can look like Audrey Hepburn by flipping out their hair, buying the large glasses and the little sleeveless dresses." Women continue to do that to this day. Fashion experts have said that Hepburn's longevity as a style icon was because she stuck with a look that suited her – "clean lines, simple yet bold accessories, minimalist palette."

In December 2009, an auction of clothing and accessories that had been worn by Audrey, and some of her personal letters, raised £270,200 ($437,000). The letters included correspondence with her fiancé

Dress by Valentino, worn by Audrey Hepburn. Photographed at the exhibition Valentino a Roma *at Museo Ara Pacis in Rome.*

James Hanson prior to their planned 1952 wedding. Also auctioned was the wedding dress, designed by the Fortuna Sisters, for her eventually cancelled wedding to Hanson. Upon deciding that she no longer needed the dress, Audrey asked that the designers give it to a bride who could use it.

Other items auctioned were the Givenchy-designed black Chantilly lace cocktail gown from the Ritz bar scene in *How to Steal a Million* (1966) and the black cloqué silk gown from *Paris When It Sizzles* (1962). The former sold for £60,000 and the latter for £16,800. Half the proceeds were donated to All Children in School, a joint venture of The Audrey Hepburn Children's Fund and UNICEF.

In 2007, the hot pink cocktail dress worn by Audrey Hepburn during the filming of Breakfast at Tiffany's *sold for $192,000.*

DEATH

In 1992, after her last trip for UNICEF to the country of Somalia, Audrey began suffering abdominal pains. She visited specialists in Switzerland, but was not diagnosed until she went to Cedars Sinai in Los Angeles, California, in October 1992. In early November, Audrey was finally deemed to have abdominal cancer that had spread from her appendix, a very rare form of cancer. The cancer, after growing for several years, had metastasized as a thin coating over her small intestine, strangling her small intestine and causing it to spasm. There was time for only one chemotherapy treatment before an obstruction required Audrey to undergo more surgery on December 1. In less than one hour, the surgeon determined that the cancer had spread so aggressively that there was nothing more to be done.

After coming to terms with the gravity of Audrey's illness, she and her family chose to return to Switzerland to celebrate her last Christmas. The flight home was dangerous for Audrey because the change in cabin pressure on take-off and landing could possibly burst the multiple occlusions in her intestine, which might then ultimately result in a quick death from toxemia. Coming to her aid, Hubert de Givenchy arranged for a private jet, a more controlled way to deal with the dangers of flying, to take Audrey from Los Angeles to Geneva, where she and her traveling companions arrived on December 20, 1992.

In his memoir about his mother, *Audrey Hepburn, An Elegant Spirt,* Sean Ferrer recounts his mother's last month in her beloved home in Switzerland. There Audrey was surrounded by family and friends, although she had said her final good-bye to her best friend, Connie Wald, when she left Los Angeles.

Audrey, although weak, was well enough to meander again through her garden, one of her favorite places on earth. A testament to Audrey's undying ability to fascinate the public, she was unfortunately dogged by paparazzi even as she strolled in her garden sanctuary. As she nurtured her garden in life, Audrey left instructions regarding the care of her garden's trees, shrubs, and flowers in the years that would follow after her death.

Audrey Hepburn's Star on The Hollywood Walk of Fame is located at 1650 Vine Street.

Although unable to eat because of the cancer strangling her intestines, Audrey did participate in the holiday festivities during the Christmas celebration of 1992. As her gift, Audrey created a poem that was derived from a letter written by the author Sam Levenson to his granddaughter on the day of her birth. Audrey read her poem to the family, close friends, and caregivers who shared the holiday with her in Switzerland. She called the poem "Time-Tested Beauty Tips." The poem is reprinted on page 84 of this book.

Quietly and peacefully, Audrey died in her sleep in the early evening of January 20, 1993, at her home of 30 years, La Paisible, in Tolochenaz in the canton of Vaud in Switzerland. She was unattended at the moment of her death, but not alone. Her loved ones were never far away and had kept constant vigil in her last days.

She spoke her last words to her son Sean the night before she died, awakening briefly from sleep. According to Sean, he asked her if she had any regrets. Audrey's response was that she was sorry not to have met the Dalai Lama because "he was the closest thing to God we have on earth."

Her 30-minute funeral service was held at the small Protestant church in the village of Tolochenaz, Switzerland, on January 24, 1993, and was attended by 600 mourners. Maurice Eindiguer, the same pastor who wed Hepburn and Mel Ferrer and baptized their son Sean in 1960, presided over her funeral. Prince Sadruddin Aga Khan, representing UNICEF, delivered a eulogy.

Many family members and friends attended the funeral, including her sons, Sean Ferrer and Luca Doti, her partner Robert Wolders, her brother Ian Quarles von Ufford, ex-husbands Andrea Dotti and Mel Ferrer, her close friend Hubert de Givenchy, executives of UNICEF, and fellow actors Alain Delon and Roger Moore.

The day of her funeral, Audrey was interred in a delicate pine coffin at the Tolochenaz Cemetery, a small cemetery that sits atop a hill overlooking the village of the same name.

On December 5, 2006, Audrey Hepburn's "little black dress" from Breakfast at Tiffany's *sold for a record-breaking £467,200.*

BIBLIOGRAPHY

Many thanks to the official Audrey Hepburn website (www.audreyhepburn.com) for important details regarding Audrey's life and her sweeping contributions to 20th-century culture, style, and humanitarianism.

"Audrey Hepburn: Style Icon." BBC News, May 4, 2004.

"Audrey Hepburn's Little Black Dress Tops Fashion List." *The Independent*, May 17, 2010.

Connolly, Mike. "Who Needs Beauty!" *Photoplay*, January 1954.

Dahl, Melissa. "Stylebook: Hepburn Gown Fetches Record Price." *Pittsburgh Post-Gazette*, December 11, 2006.

Erwin, Ellen, & Jessica Diamond. *The Audrey Hepburn Treasures*. New York: Simon & Schuster

Ferrer, Sean. *Audrey Hepburn, An Elegant Spirit*. New York: Atria Books, 2003.
Harris, Warren. *Audrey Hepburn: A Biography*. New York: Simon & Schuster, 1994.

Higham, Charles. *Audrey: The Life of Audrey Hepburn*. New York: MacMillan, 1984.

Kane, Chris. "Breakfast at Tiffany's." *Screen Stories*, December 1961.

Lane, Megan. "Audrey Hepburn: Why the Fuss?" *BBC News Magazine*, April 7, 2006.

Maychick, Diana. *Audrey Hepburn: An Intimate Portrait*. New York: Birch Lane Press, 1993.

"The Most Famous Dresses Ever." Glamour.com, April 2007.

Nichols, Mark. "Audrey Hepburn Goes Back to the Bar." *Coronet,* November 1956.

Wasson, Sam. *Fifth Avenue, 5AM: Audrey Hepburn, Breakfast at Tiffany's, and the Dawn of the American Woman*. New York: Harper Collins, 2010.

Audrey's grave in Tolochenaz, Switzerland, (credit: Alexandra Spürk) July 11, 2008.